Breathing Strong

By Vikki McIntyre
Illustrated by Mila Aydingoz

We respect and honour Aboriginal and Torres Strait Islander Elders past, present and future. We acknowledge the stories, traditions and living cultures of Aboriginal and Torres Strait Islander peoples on this land and commit to building a brighter future together.

Library For All Ltd.

Understanding respiratory health

When we breathe easily, we don't really think about it. But breathing problems, like asthma and bronchitis, can make everyday life difficult. For our mob, respiratory illnesses are common.

We can care for ourselves using both western medicines and traditional bush medicines.

'Respiratory' means our body's breathing system.

How breathing works

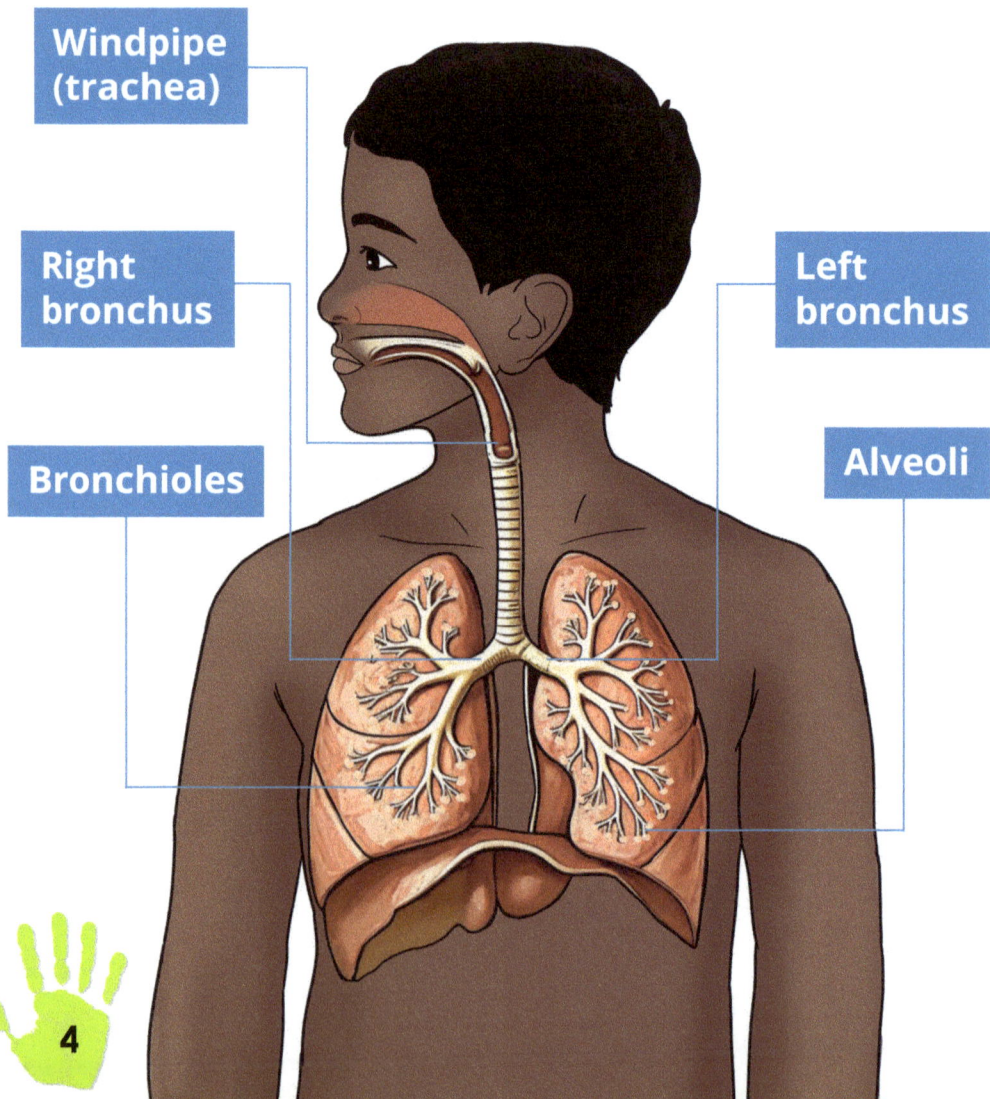

Windpipe
(trachea)

Right
bronchus

Bronchioles

Left
bronchus

Alveoli

Breathing is one of the most important things people do. It keeps us alive. We breathe through both our nose and our mouth, filling and emptying our lungs.

Breathing in brings oxygen into our lungs, while breathing out releases carbon dioxide. Our blood carries oxygen from our lungs through the rest of our body and returns carbon dioxide to our lungs to be exhaled. The gases are exchanged inside the lungs through tiny blood vessels. Everything in our body needs oxygen to function.

What are asthma and bronchitis?

Normal lung

Normal airway

Normal airway wall

Relaxed airway smooth muscle

Asthmatic lung

Constricted airway

Mucus hypersection

Thickened and inflamed airway wall

Tightened airway smooth muscle

Asthma and bronchitis share a lot of the same symptoms.

DID YOU KNOW?

Asthma makes breathing difficult. It can feel like trying to breathe through a thin straw. People with asthma sometimes cough, wheeze or feel tightness in their chest.

Bronchitis causes swelling in the breathing tubes, which can lead to a cough that may produce mucus.

These conditions happen for many reasons, including allergies, smoke from fires, dust and germs.

Staying healthy means knowing how to use western and bush medicines together.

How bush medicines can help us

Our mob has used bush medicines for thousands of years. Many plants found on Country can help with breathing problems.

Eucalyptus (gum tree): The leaves help clear blocked noses and ease coughs. Breathing in steam from eucalyptus oil mixed in hot water can open your lungs and help you breathe easier.

Lemon myrtle: These leaves can be boiled into a tea that soothes a sore throat and helps fight chest infections. You can find lemon myrtle in rainforest areas along the east coast.

Native lemongrass: Used to help with coughs and colds, native lemongrass can be brewed into tea, helping reduce inflammation in your throat and lungs. It grows in grasslands and open forests.

Tea tree (Melaleuca): Oil from tea tree leaves helps fight infections because it kills germs. You can breathe it in as steam or apply it mixed into creams. It mostly grows along streams and swamps.

Umbrella bush wattle: The bark and leaves can be soaked or boiled to make a sticky gum that helps with sore throats and coughs. You can find this plant in every state of Australia.

Cultural connections

Using bush medicines makes our cultural connections stronger and helps pass important knowledge down through generations.

Our Elders can teach us how to identify, gather, and prepare these plants safely and respectfully. Learning about these medicines can be fun and rewarding, bringing families together and keeping important traditions alive.

Western medicines that help your lungs

Doctors can also give us strong and fast-acting medicines for asthma and bronchitis.

Asthma inhalers (Ventolin) quickly open airways, helping to breathe easier right away.

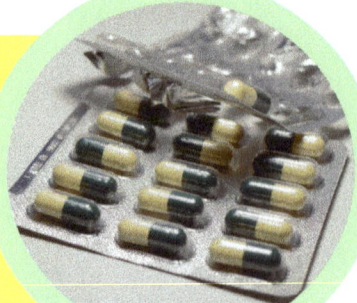

Antibiotics (like Amoxicillin) fight bacteria that cause chest infections and bronchitis.

Steroid medicine (like Flixotide) reduces swelling in your lungs, helping prevent asthma attacks.

Cough medicine helps stop constant coughing, making rest easier.

Our mob way

Using bush medicines and western medicines together can help you breathe even better. Here's how you can combine them safely:

- If you have asthma, always use your inhaler first if you feel tightness or shortness of breath. Afterwards, breathing in steam with eucalyptus oil can soothe your lungs and help breathing stay comfortable longer.
- When you have bronchitis, antibiotics from your doctor are important to clear infections quickly. Drinking lemon myrtle or native lemongrass tea can comfort your throat, reduce coughing, and help you feel stronger.

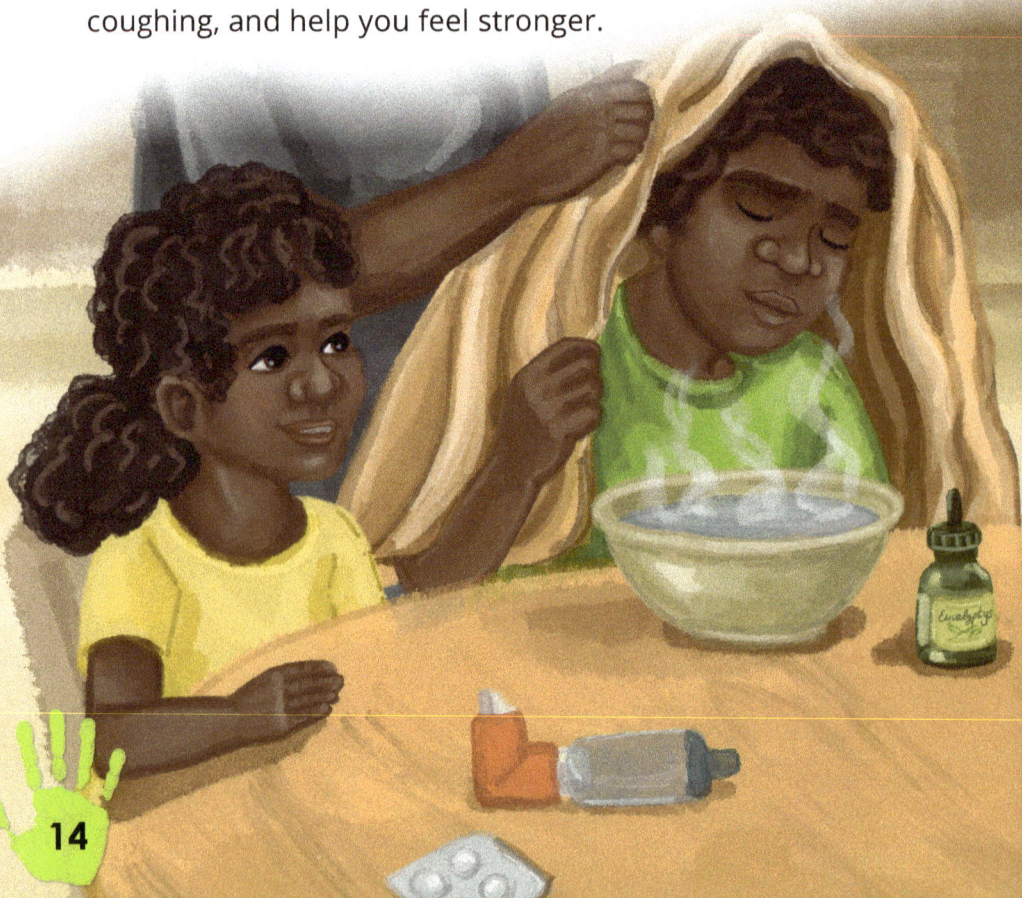

- If your chest feels tight or sore from coughing, tea tree oil breathed in as steam or rubbed gently on your chest can help reduce discomfort. But keep using your inhaler because it stops your lungs from swelling and keeps you safe from future asthma attacks.

Looking after your lungs for the future

It's important to take care of your lungs now. If you smoke or don't look after your lungs, you could be at risk of developing serious conditions like chronic obstructive pulmonary disease (COPD) or pneumonia later in life. Some of our Elders and older mob struggle with these diseases.

COPD makes breathing very hard and can cause long-term lung damage.

Pneumonia is a serious lung infection, especially dangerous for older people or those with weaker lungs.

You can also talk to your doctor or nurse about staying on top of your vaccinations, especially for things like the flu, which can affect your lungs. Healthy eating and exercise are also good ways to look after your lungs, and your whole body.

Caring for your lungs today helps you stay healthy and deadly tomorrow.

Caring for Country, caring for your health

Bush medicine connects us to culture, ancestors, and our land and island homes. Using these traditional bush medicines along with western medicines keeps both our body and spirit strong.

Knowing how to use both kinds of medicines means you can breathe easy and stay strong.

REMEMBER!

Don't pick any plants or make any bush medicines without an adult who knows what plants are safe and how to prepare them.

Always talk with Elders, your family, or health workers about using bush medicines safely.

Photo Credits

Page	Attribution
Page 5	Caro Telfer/austockphoto.com.au
Page 8 (eucalyptus)	abeldomi/pixabay.com
Page 9 (lemon myrtle)	lynnebeclu/istockphoto.com
Page 9 (lemongrass)	y-studio/istockphoto.com
Page 9 (tea tree)	narvikk/istockphoto.com
Page 9 (umbrella bush wattle)	PublicDomainPictures/pixabay.com
Pages 10–11	xavierarnau/istockphoto.com
Page 12 (inhaler)	coltsfan/pixabay.com
Page 12 (antibiotics)	AKuptsova/pixabay.com
Page 13 (steroid)	Laboko/istockphoto.com
Page 13 (cough medicine)	ds_30/pixabay.com
Pages 16–17	AlexanderFord/istockphoto.com

You can use these questions to talk about this book with your family, friends and teachers.

What did you learn from this book?

Describe this book in one word.
Funny? Scary? Colourful? Interesting?

How did this book make you feel when you finished reading it?

What was your favourite part of this book?

Download the Library For All Reader app from
libraryforall.org

About the author

Vikki McIntyre was born in Sydney and grew up in the western suburbs. Her ancestral Country is the south coast of New South Wales. She descends from the saltwater people of the Dharawal language group. Vikki is happiest when she can feel sand under her feet and smell saltwater in the air.

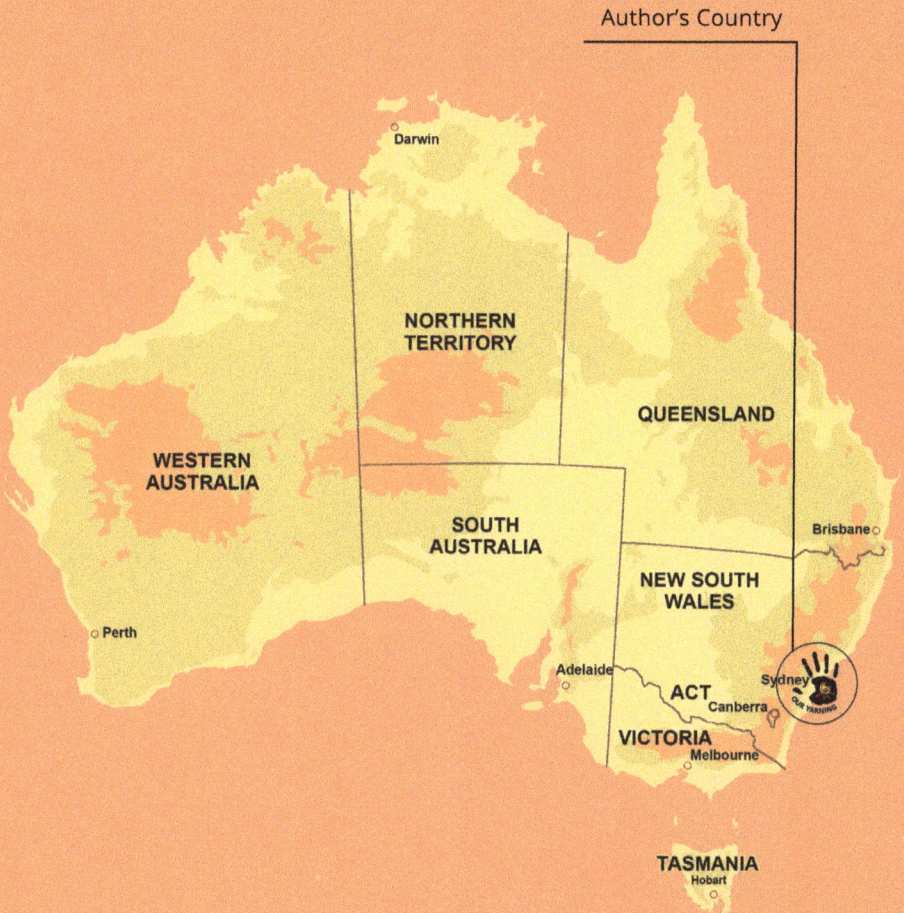

Author's Country

Darwin

NORTHERN
TERRITORY

QUEENSLAND

WESTERN
AUSTRALIA

SOUTH
AUSTRALIA

Brisbane

NEW SOUTH
WALES

Perth

Adelaide

Sydney

ACT
Canberra

VICTORIA
Melbourne

TASMANIA
Hobart

Our Yarning

The Our Yarning collection aligns with the Australian Curriculum through the Cross-Curriculum Priorities — Aboriginal and Torres Strait Islander Histories and Cultures. The collection provides an authentic opportunity for learning and embedding Aboriginal and Torres Strait Islander perspectives because it is written by Aboriginal and Torres Strait Islander people.

We know that children learn better, and enjoy reading more, when they see themselves in the stories, characters and illustrations of the books they read.

To download the app, visit the Google Play Store or Apple Store and search 'Our Yarning'.

libraryforall.org

You're reading Upper Primary

Learner – Beginner readers

Start your reading journey with short words,
big ideas and plenty of pictures.

Level 1 – Rising readers

Raise your reading level with more words,
simple sentences and exciting images.

Level 2 – Eager readers

Enjoy your reading time with familiar words,
but complex sentences.

Level 3 – Progressing readers

Develop your reading skills with creative stories
and some challenging vocabulary.

Level 4 – Fluent readers

Step up your reading skills with playful narratives,
new words and fun facts.

Middle Primary – Curious readers

Discover your world through science and stories.

Upper Primary – Adventurous readers

Explore your world through science and stories.

LIBRARY FOR ALL

DIGITAL EDUCATION · FOR THE WORLD

Library For All is an Australian not for profit organisation with a mission to make knowledge accessible to all via an innovative digital library solution. Visit us at libraryforall.org

Breathing Strong

First published 2025

Published by Library For All Ltd
Email: info@libraryforall.org
URL: libraryforall.org

This book was made possible by the generous contributions of GSK.

gsk

Our Yarning logo design by Jason Lee, Bidjipidji Art

Original illustrations by Mila Aydingoz

Breathing Strong
McIntyre, Vikki
ISBN: 978-1-923554-99-3
SKU04961

www.ingramcontent.com/pod-product-compliance
Lightning Source LLC
Chambersburg PA
CBHW042343040426
42448CB00019B/3384